DOTHEBOYS AND BOWES

THE YORKSHIRE SCHOOLS
AND THEIR PLACE IN THE HISTORY OF EDUCATION

By ALAN WILKINSON

The internal economy of Dotheboys Hall

Published by Mosaic (Teesdale) Ltd for
Dickens in Teesdale
to celebrate the 200th anniversary of the birth of
Charles Dickens, 7th February 1812

ISBN 978 0 956781 63 5

© Alan Wilkinson 2012

Cover design and photograph of the author by Stuart Short

Book design by Mosaic (Teesdale) Ltd,
Moor Edge, Snaisgill, Middleton-in-Teesdale, County Durham DL12 0RP

Set in 11/14 Caslon Pro. Typeset by Mosaic (Teesdale) Ltd

Published by Mosaic (Teesdale) Ltd, for Dickens in Teesdale, part of the
Mid-Teesdale Project Partnership (registered charity number 111 8591),
with the support of:

Teesdale
Area Action Partnership

www.mosaicprintdesign.co.uk
www.dickensinteesdale.org.uk

Dedicated to the late J Merryne Watson,
who was generous in sharing his knowledge.

Acknowledgements

Members of the Dickens in Teesdale group, led by Sandra Moorhouse and Peter Gilbertson, all of whom are volunteers, have been very supportive during the writing of this book. I am particularly grateful to Diana Collecott for her helpful suggestions on the final draft; she and Caroline Peacock kindly co-operated in preparing the text for the printer. I enjoyed working with Stuart Short who took the colour photographs. Gratitude is due to the Heritage Lottery Fund and Teesdale Action Partnership for the grants that made this publication possible.

I wish to thank the Trustees of the Dickens House Museum in London for permission to reproduce the portrait of Charles Dickens by Samuel Lawrence, and the Headmasters of West Buckland School and Barnard Castle School for permission to use pictures of their school buildings as illustrations. Thanks are also due to the current owners of other properties photographed for this book, to Stuart Short who designed the cover and to Judith Mashiter, who designed the book at short notice and oversaw its production.

Alan Wilkinson, February 2012

Contents

List of illustrations

Charles Dickens, aged 25 in 1837, shortly before he came to Teesdale

1

Enter Charles Dickens

As we came further north, the snow grew deeper. At about eight o'Clock, it began to fall heavily, and as we crossed the wild heaths hereabout, there was no vestige of a track... at eleven we reached a bare place with a house standing alone in the midst of a dreary moor, which the Guard informed us was Greta Bridge.

That was written by Charles Dickens, in a letter to his wife dated Thursday 1st February 1838. He had travelled by stagecoach from London to Teesdale over the past two days, having been on the road for twenty-nine hours at an average speed of eight and a half miles an hour. Especially in such inclement weather as he had endured, coach travel was a severe ordeal.

Dickens was travelling with the artist who illustrated some of his books, Hablot K Browne. The two men were visiting Teesdale to investigate the notorious boarding schools of North Yorkshire, which were to be satirised in the form of Dotheboys Hall in Dickens' projected novel, *The Life and Adventures of Nicholas Nickleby*.

It was not a cheerful mission. It had been a tedious journey and when the two travellers eventually alighted at the coaching inn, they were cold, tired and in what Dickens called "an agony of apprehension", for there were no signs of anybody being up in the house. However, their fears were soon dispelled when they were served with a hot supper and a bottle of mulled port before retiring to their bedrooms, in each of which was, Dickens reported, "a rousing fire halfway up the chimney."

Next day, fortified by an enormous breakfast (even allowing for Dickens' occasional tendency to exaggerate) the author and his illustrator set off for Barnard Castle, some four miles away along a minor road. Here, he and Browne booked accommodation for two nights at the King's Head. Using this inn as a base from which to conduct his enquiries, Dickens now began in earnest his investigations into the Yorkshire schools.

Dickens had brought with him some letters of introduction which he could present to local people who might be able to help him in his quest. These letters were not entirely honest: they referred to an imaginary widow who was thinking of sending her son to a school in Yorkshire, and who would be glad if the person receiving the letter would give her friend (i.e. Dickens) some information about such a school. Dickens said later that he thought the letter gave Browne's name rather than his own, referring to the whole scheme as a "pious fraud."

One of the letters was delivered to a local solicitor, Richard Barnes, whose office was in the Market Place opposite the King's Head. Barnes visited Dickens at the King's Head in the evening, having walked through the snow from his house in Galgate, one of the main streets of the town. He seems to have mentioned one or two schools in the district, without making a definite recommendation.

At first, Barnes was evasive when speaking of the Yorkshire schools and, while they shared some wine, preferred to talk of other topics. Eventually, however, he burst out with the information that the widow must not send her little boy to one of those schoolmasters: he would be better off holding horses' heads while their owners were elsewhere, and then, after his day's work, sleeping in the gutter. Barnes said he didn't want to speak badly about his neighbours, but would not be able to lie comfortably in his bed if he did not tell the truth.

Dickens also interviewed a man who had previously worked as an assistant teacher to William Shaw, who ran an academy at Bowes, a village four miles west of Barnard Castle. This teacher, Thomas MacKay, had parted company with Shaw and had set up his own school, a much smaller establishment, in Barnard Castle.

Dickens now had an address to visit, so he and Browne went together up the old Roman road to Bowes; there they met William Shaw, proprietor of the school described in its advertisement as 'Bowes Academy, near Greta Bridge in Yorkshire'. It is not known whether or not they went into the school, but Dickens certainly gathered a great deal of information indirectly, for in his journal he wrote:

> *Shaw, the schoolmaster we saw today, is the man in whose school several boys went blind some time since, from gross neglect. The case was tried, and the verdict went against him. It must have been between 1823 and 1826. Look this out in the newspapers.*

The case against Shaw was, in fact, heard in the Court of Common Pleas in 1823, and revealed far more about Bowes Academy than the actual neglect of boys suffering from some form of ophthalmic disease. In giving his evidence, one boy, William Jones, spoke of his experiences at the school, including details of the pupils' diet. They had 'hasty pudding' (flour stirred in milk or water, to the consistency of thick batter) for breakfast; at main meals meat was served three times a week, and on other days they had potatoes and bread and cheese. At tea-time the boys had warm watered milk and bread; there was no supper.

On Sundays, they had "skimmings of the pot". How long the pot had been simmering, or allowed to cool before being reheated, is not stated, but there were maggots in the mixture. A teacher, said Jones, had told the boys that they could have a penny if they could fill a mug with maggots; they filled a quart pot but received no money.

The boys slept on mattresses filled with hay and straw, four or five boys shared a bed and there were about thirty beds in each room. There were fleas in the beds, and the boys were told to remove them by using a quill pen. The broad end of the quill was cut off and the hollow end had to be quickly put over any flea which the boys saw; the flea then leapt up into the quill and was captured. The witness said that boys were beaten if they did not perform this task. They washed at a trough in the school yard and there were only two towels. (Jones had earlier stated that the school had three hundred pupils.) Each dormitory had a large tub in the middle instead of chamber pots.

Before considering how Dickens made use of some of these facts when he began to write *Nicholas Nickleby*, some explanation is needed to amplify the assertions made by William Jones. The school itself was, and still is, the last house at the western end of the village of Bowes. Despite its long frontage, facing onto the garden, it does not look as if it could readily accommodate three hundred boys, together with assistant masters and the proprietor's own family. The explanation is that one large wing of the building has since been demolished.

William Shaw's Academy at Bowes as it is today, seen from the garden

An artist's impression of Shaw's Academy in 1838, before the south wing was demolished; inset, the pump at which the pupils washed

Two towels for three hundred boys seems incredible, but could well account for the rapid spread of the eye infection which was the subject of the trial. A former pupil at Woden Croft, a school between Cotherstone and Romaldkirk, recalled, "We had not any towels and had to dry ourselves with our garments." The large tub for the use of so many boys in one room was not a unique arrangement. Male factory workers in Kidderminster, for example, used a large communal tub during working hours; this was a useful custom because human urine was a significant ingredient in fixing dyes in the wool from which carpets were made. Hygiene was of a much lower standard in those days.

Such details as the nocturnal use of a large tub in dormitories were avoided by Dickens, who was conscious of writing for a mixed readership of men, women and children of various ages. Other topics mentioned in the court case did, however, find their way onto the pages of *Nicholas Nickleby*. In Chapter Four, for example, the watered milk mentioned in court is transferred to the coffee room of the Saracen's Head in London before the new boys set off for Dotheboys Hall, the fictitious school in

Bowes. In the novel, the schoolmaster, Mr Wackford Squeers, tells the waiter who brings a mug with some milk in it to fill it up with lukewarm water.

In Chapter Seven, the topic of the number of boys sharing one bed is transferred from the courtroom to Dotheboys Hall. Squeers asks his wife: "Who sleeps in Brooks's bed, my dear?" The exchange continues as follows:

> "In Brooks's," said Mrs Squeers, pondering. "There's Jennings, little Bolder, Graymarsh, and what's his name."
>
> "So there is," rejoined Squeers. "Yes! Brooks's is full."

This detail agrees exactly with William Jones' evidence that four or five boys shared a bed. Similarly, Squeers makes it clear that towels are shared when he says to Nicholas at bedtime, "I don't know, I am sure, whose towel to put you on; but if you'll make shift with something tomorrow morning, Mrs Squeers will arrange that, in the course of the day." In fact, the arrangement of washing at an open-air trough has to be postponed on the first morning, because the pump is frozen. "So," says Squeers, "you must be content with giving yourself a dry polish."

The main point of Shaw's trial in the Court of Common Pleas was, however, his alleged neglect of the boys. The facts are grim, but Dickens gives them no place in the novel; they do, however, add to the impression of life in one of the Yorkshire schools.

William Jones said that one October he felt that his eyes were weak and he could not do his work on his copy book, from which he was meant to learn how to write clearly; he was threatened with a beating; on the next day he could not see at all. He was sent with three other boys to an outhouse, and said he stayed there a month, by which time there were eighteen boys in the outhouse. He was then moved to another room, which contained nine boys who were blind.

The jury reached a verdict against Shaw, who had to pay £300 damages. On the following day, a similar case was brought against him. In this case, a Mr Ockerby said that in 1820 three sons of his had gone to Shaw's school where, by September, two were badly affected by the eye disease and were later unable to read or write; one boy lost the use of one eye and another boy was affected for life. After only one witness had been heard, Shaw's lawyer agreed to accept the same verdict and and the damages that had been decided in the previous day's case.

The ophthalmic infection is not referred to in the novel as one of the dangers to which the pupils were exposed, but the fictitious schoolmaster himself is handicapped by having only one eye; his other eye is also affected, making him ugly in appearance. If the schoolboys had suffered in this way in the novel, the topic would have been sympathetically dealt with. Since it is Mr Squeers, the object of Dickens' satire, who is afflicted, the novelist's description is expressed in an unpleasantly humorous way. In Chapter Four, he says of the schoolmaster:

> Mr Squeers's appearance was not prepossessing. He had but one eye, and the popular prejudice runs in favour of two. The eye he had was unquestionably useful, but decidedly not ornamental, being of a greenish grey, and in shape resembling the fanlight of a street door.

It appears, then, that almost all the defects of life at Dotheboys Hall are created from details which Dickens learned from evidence reported at the trial of William Shaw. That gave him the basis for the inadequate diet, the crowded and unhygienic living conditions and the constant threat of beatings, which were all daily features of the lives of pupils at Dotheboys. Essentially, Dickens already had enough material in his mind to form the basis of the early chapters of *The Life and Adventures of Nicholas Nickleby*.

However, Dickens' and Browne's visit to Bowes provided two other important ingredients of the novel. In addition to being a boarding school, Shaw's property was also a farm. Farming was all part of the profitable business run by many of the Yorkshire schoolmasters. At Dotheboys Hall, as a fictitious example of reality, the farm is sometimes in the forefront of the schoolmaster's mind. This is demonstrated in Chapter Seven, when Wackford Squeers greets his wife after he has been absent in London for some days; the conversation is begun by his wife:

"How is my Squeery?" said this lady in a playful manner.

"Quite well, my love," replied Squeers. "How's the cows?"

"All right, every one of 'em," answered the lady.

"And the pigs?" said Squeers.

"As well as they were when you went away."

"Come; that's a blessing," said Squeers, pulling off his great-coat.
"The boys are well as they were, I suppose?"

"Oh yes, they're well enough," replied Mrs Squeers, snappishly.

Mr Squeers' first enquiry is about the farm's livestock; it is an example of the maxim which he quoted to a new boy when he said in Chapter Four, "'Never postpone business' is the first lesson we instil into our commercial pupils." Squeers practises what he preaches and checks his business assets before enquiring after the well-being of his clients.

Presumably Dickens noticed the farm buildings and the adjacent grazing land while he was in Bowes visiting Shaw's Academy, and drew the correct conclusion. Since Squeers' educational system included receiving unpaid household help from the pupils, it is reasonable to suppose that the boys also acted from time to time as farm labourers. This certainly did occur at Bowes Hall, a school at the other end of the village, which Dickens and Browne passed on their journey to and from Barnard Castle. All that the novel reveals, however, is that the boys at Dotheboys helped with household tasks.

The following passage, in Chapter Eight, occurs when Squeers is introducing Nicholas to the school's educational system:

"This is the first class in English spelling and philosophy, Nickleby," said Squeers, beckoning Nicholas to stand beside him. "We'll get up a Latin one, and hand that over to you. Now, then, where's the first boy?"

"Please, sir, he's cleaning the back parlour window," said the temporary head of the philosophical class.

"So he is, to be sure," rejoined Squeers. "We go upon the practical mode of teaching, Nickleby; the regular education system. C-l-e-a-n, clean, verb active, to make bright, to scour. W-i-n, win, d-e-r, der, winder, a casement. When the boy knows this out of a book, he goes and does it. It's just the same principle as the use of globes."

On a similar principle, another boy is weeding the garden, and a third one is rubbing down Squeers' horse. Class is then dismissed so that other boys can draw water from the well, for the next day is washing day and the coppers need to be filled to heat the water.

Of all the characters in *Nicholas Nickleby*, and indeed in all of Dickens' work, Smike is one of the most well-known; Smike is a pitiable figure, psychologically and physically afflicted by the cruel treatment which he receives at the hands of Mr and Mrs Squeers, for whom he acts as an unpaid servant. He is also abandoned or disregarded by everyone, until he is befriended by Nicholas. Later it becomes clear that Smike is central to the development of the plot.

All of those circumstances are created by Dickens' own inventive imagination, but the starting point for creating the character of Smike was provided by Dickens' and Browne's explorations at Bowes on the cold and gloomy afternoon of Friday 2nd February 1838. Dickens gave an account of the moment at which he thought that the concept of Smike first came into his mind. He had entered the churchyard by the easterly of two gates leading from the Back Lane, and he saw on his left a headstone at the grave of a former pupil. The inscription reads:

HERE lie
the Remains of
GEORGE ASHTON TAYLOR
Son of John Taylor
of Trowbridge Wilts
who died suddenly at
MR WILLIAM SHAWS ACADEMY
of this place April 13th 1822
Aged 19 Years
Young reader thou must die
But after this the Judgement

George Ashton Taylor's headstone in Bowes Churchyard

Dickens wrote about this discovery in a letter, dated 29th December 1838, to the writer and philanthropist, Anna Maria Hall. Mrs Hall had sent Dickens an anecdote relating to William Shaw; his reply to her included the following detail about his visit to Bowes:

> *The country for miles around was covered, when I was there, with deep snow. There is an old Church near the School, and the first grave-stone I stumbled on that dreary afternoon was placed above the grave of a boy, eighteen long years old, who had died—suddenly, the inscription said; I suppose his heart broke—the Camel falls down 'suddenly' when they heap the last load upon his back—died at that wretched place. I think his ghost put Smike into my head, upon the spot.*

Dickens' suppositions about the reasons for the lad's death are without foundation: they are the basis for fiction. Nevertheless, when Smike is first described, there are echoes of both the gravestone and the feelings expressed in the letter to Mrs Hall. In Chapter Eight, Dickens writes of Smike: "He could not have been less than eighteen or nineteen years old." In the next chapter, when Nicholas speaks comfortingly to Smike, the poor wretch bursts into tears and cries, "Oh dear, oh dear! My heart will break. It will, it will."

One more phenomenon from Bowes directly affected the novel: this was the character of Wackford Squeers. It is unclear how much contact the visitors had with Shaw and, therefore, how much of his character can be traced in Wackford Squeers. They share the initials 'W S', which might well be significant. If it does not suggest that the real schoolmaster and the fictitious one are connected, then Dickens was very careless in not choosing different initials.

As far as Dickens' own testimony goes, the character of Wackford Squeers is not suggestive of any one man but is rather to be taken as representative of a species. In his Preface to the first edition of *Nicholas Nickleby* he says, "Squeers is a representative of a class, and not of an individual." He then relates that more than one Yorkshire schoolmaster laid claim to being the original of Squeers: one had taken advice on a possible legal action; one had threatened to commit assault and battery on the author; another (who sounds as if he had some knowledge of Dickens' and Browne's explorations) said he remembered that one visitor had held him in conversation, while another had "taken his likeness." Dickens dismisses these claims by writing, in his Preface to the novel:

> Where imposture, ignorance, and brutal cupidity, are the stock in trade of a small body of men, and one is described by these characteristics, all his friends will recognise something belonging to themselves, and each will have a misgiving that the portrait is his own.

One essential ingredient in the presentation of Dotheboys Hall was apparently not based on what Dickens learned from his visit to Bowes. He heard of threats of beating, but not of how horrifyingly cruel the beatings were. In Chapter Eight examples abound, and Squeers himself refers to them as "thrashings." An example is made of the pupil Bolder: "Wholly disregarding a piteous cry for mercy, Mr Squeers fell upon the boy and caned him soundly, not leaving off, indeed, until his arm was tired out." Another child is beaten by Squeers, until, "the little urchin in his writhings actually rolled out of his hands."

Possibly the cruellest beating of all was reserved for Smike. This comes in Chapter Thirteen, as a punishment for running away from the school: after one blow from Squeers and a scream of pain from Smike, Nicholas intervenes and calls on Squeers to stop. In his fury at Nicholas, Squeers "struck him a blow across the face with his instrument of torture", at which "Nicholas sprang upon him, wrested the weapon from his hand and, pinning him by the throat, beat the ruffian till he roared for mercy".

It is probable that Dickens had no need to stimulate his imagination by learning details of savage beatings at Bowes, for his own childhood experiences had given him plenty of material. Part of his education was provided by a school called Wellington House Academy, in London, where the headmaster, a Mr William Jones, was remembered by one of his pupils as having "an undoubted love of the cane." Dickens seems to have used Mr Jones as the model for Mr Creakle in *David Copperfield*. In Chapter Six of that novel, Dickens writes that, as well as using the cane, Creakle took a "delight in cuffing the boys, which was like the satisfying of a craving appetite."

Such remarks suggest a degree of sadism; certainly there is something unwholesome in the gusto with which Squeers attacks the boys. Before beginning to chastise Smike, Squeers gives his "right arm two or three flourishes to try its power and suppleness", and tells his wife, "Stand a little out of the way, Mrs Squeers, my dear, I've hardly got room enough." It is no wonder that Mr Richard Barnes, the solicitor of Barnard Castle, advised Dickens not to let the hypothetical widow send her little boy to the care of such schoolmasters.

2

Some tales out of school

Dickens and Browne stayed for two nights in Barnard Castle before they set off for Darlington, where they boarded the coach to York, and then another for London. There, Dickens was re-united with his wife and their first-born son. In the letter to his wife from Greta Bridge, he had pictured the baby "crawling about the floor of this Yorkshire inn", and added, "Bless his heart, I would give two sovereigns for a kiss."

Following their reunion, Dickens soon settled down to write his new novel which, as usual, was to be published in serial form. On 7th February, his twenty-sixth birthday, he told John Forster (later to be his biographer), "I have begun! I wrote four slips last night, so you see the beginning is made. And what is more, I can go on."

After only two full days in Teesdale he had gathered enough information to feel confident that he could write about one fictitious "Yorkshire school" and make it representative of all such schools. Once the topic had been introduced into the early instalments of the novel, various people sent him further information about the schools, which supported his own feelings about them. Research, recorded memories and new information (not all of it condemnatory) continued to be published throughout the nineteenth and twentieth centuries and still appears today. Some related to schools that Dickens may never have heard of, while other material featured schools very near to where he had made his enquiries.

Bowes Hall, formerly Clarkson's Academy, now a private residence

One such example, already mentioned, was the school at Bowes Hall, at the eastern end of the village. T P Cooper, in his book *With Dickens in Yorkshire*, records that window panes were scribbled with names of former pupils dating from a hundred years earlier. There were other inscriptions including the lines: "I know a maid who doth possess / An elegance of mind as well as dress"; another, more down-to-earth, reads: "Money like manure is of no use unless it is spread."

The latter inscription, like the philosophy of Dotheboys Hall, unites commercial education with agricultural labour; an old pupil remembered that an assistant teacher at Bowes Hall did sometimes say, "Now, lads, we'll have a day off and go and spread muck." From time to time, the 'day off' was occupied with chopping wood, hay making, and even carrying stones from a quarry for repairing field walls or farm buildings.

Bowes Hall school was run by a Mr Clarkson and (according to its advertisement) "his able assistants". Clarkson died in 1838, the year of Dickens' visit to the village, but his widow and daughter carried on the business. There were other schools of a similar nature in Bowes. A former Clerk to the Barnard Castle Local Board of Health and to its successor, the Urban District Council, wrote in his autobiography that there were four such schools in the village, and traced another nine "within an easy radius" of Barnard Castle. The author was J Ingram Dawson, in his autobiography, *Reminiscences of a Rascally Lawyer.*

Dawson was born in 1862 and educated at Gainford Academy, a reputable school between Barnard Castle and Darlington, run by the Reverend William Bowman. This headmaster personally told Dawson that, at about the middle of the nineteenth century, he heard that a school at Bowes was closing. Needing more furnishings for his own expanding school, Bowman sent his son to see if he could buy anything useful at the closing-down auction sale.

It was a very wet and windy day, so the auction, which was to have been conducted in the garden, was moved to the school dining room. The smell in there was appalling and no windows would open. The reason for the smell was soon discovered: beneath the three long tables were piles of old potato skins that had been scraped off the boys' plates along the whole length of the table, and apparently left there for a long time. The auction moved again, this time to a dormitory. The bedsteads were sold in the dormitories where they stood. They were all made of thin fir trees, roughly squared off, with laths across them to hold mattresses filled with chaff. There was nothing worth buying.

Bowman's son had a wasted day, but the story illustrates an aspect of life in a Yorkshire school that would otherwise have been unknown. The school was not actually named, but the only school, apart from William Shaw's Academy, that is mentioned by name in Dawson's book, is Bowes Hall.

This book also includes an unusual piece of information about the boys themselves. John Thompson, a tradesman in Barnard Castle, was born in 1810, so was twenty-eight years old when Dickens came to the town. In his old age he told Dawson that boys from Bowes used to come down to Barnard Castle during their spells of unoccupied time. He said they were shabbily dressed and some of them wore hats without brims, while others wore only brims on their heads. They came in hopes of making some pocket money by selling jackdaws as pets, pigeons to be cooked in pies, as well as other birds and varieties of eggs.

It is likely that these boys came from William Shaw's Academy, for a former pupil of that school said that, especially in good weather, Shaw sometimes told them to disappear for the day and only come back at night. He said that they had been known to go to a secluded gully where sheep grazed on the moor, kill a lamb, skin it and roast it as best they could in order to eat it. The man said that they prepared for this event in advance, perhaps by stealing a knife or two; they certainly took some bread with them.

Such glimpses of the activities with which the pupils filled the long hours of boredom when work was over for the day, are rare. There were no organised games or opportunities for hobbies. Usually, the only evidence for their occupation in leisure times was that they wrote their names on any available spaces. A man who knew the former dormitory wing at Shaw's Academy said that the ceiling showed many names written in the smoke of candles held by boys on the top bunks.

T P Cooper said that a lead roof on a porch at the front of a school at Startforth had names on it ranging from 1790 to 1859. The porch was removed in the latter half of the twentieth century; a man working on its removal said he had noticed the names but had not realised their significance.

Front of Startforth House, after the removal of the porch which was inscribed with pupils' names

Former school buildings across the private yard behind Startforth House

The school buildings behind the house, across a private yard, contained one window with some names and dates engraved on it; unusually, two of the names are of girls, possibly the daughters of previous proprietors of the school. Nancy Bowman has the surname of the man who sold the property, including a schoolroom, in 1790, while Ann Galland has the same surname as a later proprietor of the school. The window-pane has now been removed, but in the mid-twentieth century the owner of the house had the foresight to make a tracing of it, to preserve the names and handwriting of the young people.

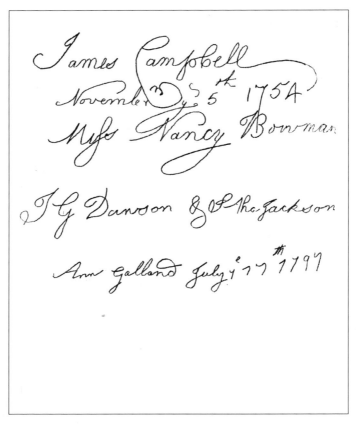

Names inscribed on a window-pane to the right of the door in the school buildings at Startforth House

At Woden Croft Academy, near Cotherstone, pupils' names were carved in stone. At that school, one of the dormitories was in the upper storey of a building separate from the house. It was approached by an outdoor staircase terminating in a stone slab in front of the door. Names and initials were carved on it, but are now almost obliterated.

Woden Croft, near Cotherstone; formerly Woden Croft Academy

*An outbuilding on the farm at Woden Croft: the first
floor was used as a school dormitory*

Woden Croft is one of the schools about which most is known, partly
because of the researches of the late J Merryne Watson, of Newsham, and

partly because of the reminiscences recorded by a former pupil named Bold Cooke, from Blackley, near Manchester, who spent "nearly four unhappy years" at Woden Croft.

Various features of Woden Croft are not mentioned in accounts of other Yorkshire schools. For example, to support the claim that this school attended strictly to the morals of the pupils, a list of twelve rules was drawn up. Here are some examples the boys were supposed to follow:

Rule 1   That they rise at 5.30 in the morning in the summer and 6.30 in the winter, dress themselves quietly and orderly and begin each day in the fear of the Lord ...

Rule 2   That they wash their hands and faces and with the utmost decency and order join in a psalm or hymn [and] devotedly attend to prayers ...

Rule 6   That they observe a solemn silence while grace is saying, eat their food decently and refrain from talking.

Rule 8   That they avoid throwing sticks or dirt, striking or teasing one another, and they are enjoined not to complain about trifles.

Rule 9   That they neither buy, sell or exchange without leave, and strictly avoid gaming.

Rule 11 That they observe a sober and becoming behaviour when going to, coming from and whilst in church or religious meeting.

The first rule, about rising early in the morning, was not unique; at another school, known as Cotherstone Academy, boys rose at 5.00am, had supper at 5.00pm, and went to bed at 7.00pm: it had been a long day. Rule 6 refers to meal-times, at which the food, according to Bold Cooke, was "mean and parsimonious". Like Dotheboys Hall, Woden Croft Academy frequently gave its pupils a sulphurous mixture known as 'brimstone and treacle', usually accompanied by a piece of brown bread at breakfast-time.

Rule 11 was a particular failure: despite attending the Wesleyan Chapel at Cotherstone on Sunday mornings and the parish church at Romaldkirk on Sunday afternoons, the boys were far from 'observing a sober and becoming behaviour' in church. While their teachers were in the pews at ground level, the pupils were in the gallery, where they amused themselves by throwing at each other the hips and haws they had collected in their pockets during their walk to church. (The pleasant rural route by fields and lanes can still be enjoyed today; Woden Croft is about equidistant from Cotherstone and Romaldkirk.)

Specific information about punishment in the schools is not often available, but a particularly harrowing incident happened at Woden Croft, related by Bold Cooke in a style that shows he personally witnessed it:

> A youth of about eighteen years ran away from school but was soon captured and ignominiously brought back. The enormity of the offence, Simpson [the headmaster] thought, required drastic punishment. To our amazement and horror, at night when we were all in bed, the poor boy was brought naked and roped to an old door into our dormitory, and was given a most heartrending thrashing before all the boys, who were told to sit up and witness the terrorising castigation. This repulsive operation, under like conditions, was repeated in each bedroom before the hapless youth was released.

One boy who ran away from Shaw's Academy at Bowes, was never recaptured: his name was Edward Smith. He made his way to the village of Woodland, twelve miles away across country, and lived in the area doing odd jobs for over thirty years until his death in 1884, when he was buried in Lynesack churchyard. In 1934 a stone kerb, paid for by public subscription, was placed round the grave, stating Edward Smith's date of death, but not his age, for he himself had not known how old he was. The inscription includes the word "Smike," in reference to the fictitious runaway in *Nicholas Nickleby*.

*A portrait, late in life, of Edward Smith who ran away
from Shaw's Academy and never returned*

To run away from a school was seen as an insult to the establishment, showing that it was unbearable to continue to live there. It was also a very poor advertisement for the school and its proprietor. In the novel, it is clear that Smike's punishment, if not stopped by Nicholas, would have been more severe than anything else done by Squeers, especially as Smike tactlessly explained his running away by saying, "I was driven to do it."

There were, however, boys who thought quite differently about their schooldays. In the grounds of Woden Croft, at a little distance from the house, there is a stone summer house, formerly in an old orchard now replanted. Over the Gothic-style entrance, is an engraved stone with a sundial and an inscription in Latin which translates as: *"Learn to live and die well* … This sun-dial was bequeathed by Thomas Branson in recognition of his gratitude for the education he received."

The former summer-house at Woden Croft: over the arch is a sundial donated by a grateful pupil

It would be interesting to know more about Thomas Branson, who attended Woden Croft from 1807 to 1815. The education may well have been of quite a high standard for intelligent pupils. If Thomas composed the inscription himself, his Latin was good, and there are other examples of well-educated pupils. Three sons of the Helmer family of Romaldkirk attended the school; two of them became doctors and the third became a solicitor. Letters from other boys educated there still exist: they are written in a clear, firm hand.

William Shaw's inscription on a book for his daughter, "Miss M A Shaw, from her Father."

Not much is known about the teachers' standards of writing, but the brief dedication by William Shaw on the fly-leaf of a book he gave to his daughter, is written in a beautiful copy-book style. It is clear that William Shaw was by no means the semi-literate man whom Dickens depicts as Wackford Squeers. Ivor Brown, an author who explored the world of Dickens, saw specimens of the work of pupils at Shaw's Academy and considered the standard of arithmetic to have been above the national average. William Shaw's great-great grandson, Edwin Shaw, has made a study of his ancestor and some of his pupils' work. The exercise books of a boy called Blanchard, who was at Shaw's school, show very neat and well-formed handwriting and figures, the latter being neatly underlined. This work suggests firm discipline and a high standard; the books are dated 1835 and 1837, shortly before Dickens' visit to Teesdale.

The most favourable picture of Shaw's school is painted by a former pupil, H F Lloyd, the Glaswegian comic actor whose autobiography was published in instalments by the *Glasgow Evening Times* in 1886. He attended Shaw's Academy for about a year and wrote of it in glowing terms. Lloyd describes Shaw himself as "a most worthy and kind-hearted, if somewhat peculiar, gentleman." He approves of Hablot K Browne's depiction of the "*outward* presentment of the man," allowing for some exaggeration. He also offers details that add conviction to the accuracy of Browne's portrait of Shaw in the person of Squeers:

Wackford Squeers with a new pupil,
as portrayed by Hablot K Browne ('Phiz')

A sharp, thin, upright little man, with a slight scale covering the pupil of one of the eyes. Yes. There he stands with his Wellington boots and short black trousers, not originally cut too short but from a habit he had of sitting with one knee over the other, and the trousers being tight, they would get 'rucked' half-way up the boots.

Lloyd goes on to give an almost lyrical description of the school's beautiful garden and its rural and historic surroundings. He writes of excellent and plentiful food, and premises kept "scrupulously clean". He also says that there were shoemakers and tailors on the premises, to keep the boys "well clad". (He points out that the £20 fees in Squeers' advertisement included clothing among the benefits promised for the boys at Dotheboys). Lloyd concludes with this description of Shaw in action:

There was less punishment for inattention than in any other

school I ever attended. Save in the way of kindness, I never, except once, knew Mr Shaw to lift his hand to a boy the whole time I was there. He would walk round the schoolroom, look over us while writing, and here and there pat a boy on the head, saying, "Good boy – good boy; you'll be a great man some day if you pay attention to your lessons." If a lad was ill, he would sit by his bed-side and play the flute… for an hour or two together to amuse him. And this was the man whom Dickens transformed into the illiterate, tyrannical, brutal pedagogue Squeers.

It should be noted that in some other parts of Lloyd's writing there are certainly inaccuracies, so aspects of his description of Shaw's Academy may well be questioned. For example, his description of the catering contrasts strongly with the evidence of the pupil who was the first witness at the Court of Common Pleas. The main point that Dickens would contest is that he transformed William Shaw directly into Wackford Squeers. It is often supposed that Shaw and Squeers are factually the same because, so far as is known, Shaw was the only proprietor whom he met, and also because he was the man against whom two court cases succeeded. However, not only did Dickens write, "Mr Squeers is the representative of a class, and not of an individual," but H F Lloyd mentions another school in the neighbourhood of the type described by Dickens:

> There, indeed, you might have found many a Smike. Boys in rags, half-starved and otherwise cruelly used, and taught scarcely anything, except hay-making, carting manure and kindred departments of industry. They were almost continuously running away and almost as regularly being caught, brought back, and frightfully punished.

To make a balanced judgement on the actual Yorkshire schools, it is helpful to know something of the standards of other schools of a different type but in the same historical period.

If the behaviour of Woden Croft boys who threw berries at each other in church seems improper to us, we may find the following account of the behaviour of pupils at Eton almost unbelievable:

> Every Sunday afternoon the headmaster attempted to read sermons to the whole school, and every Sunday afternoon the whole school shouted him down. The scenes in chapel were far from edifying: while some antique fellow doddered in the pulpit, rats would be let loose to scurry among the legs of the exploding boys.

In this account, from Lytton Strachey's book *Eminent Victorians*, the author adds that pupils at Eton lived a life of freedom mixed with terror, for after the unchecked behaviour in Sunday chapel, the boys were on Monday mornings severely beaten for making grammatical errors in their Latin lessons. The behaviour of the staff seems to have been as strange as that of the boys. Dr John Keete, headmaster from 1809 to 1834, once beat eighty boys in a single day.

Perhaps the most horrifying description of life at a school in this period comes from Charles Lamb in his *Essays of Elia*, describing life at Christ's Hospital, a charitable foundation in London. The year is 1788: about the time when some of the Yorkshire schools were being established. The topic is the familiar one of the treatment of a boy who had attempted to run away but had been recaptured. For a first offence he was made to wear fetters as he went about his ordinary life at school, so that other boys would be deterred from running away. If he repeated the offence, he was locked in a cell where a boy could just lie at full length with scarcely enough light to read by. He was fed on bread and water each day by a porter who was not allowed to speak to him. The beadle removed him twice a day to be chastised, but the boy was returned to his solitude at night. (Later, "after one or two instances of lunacy, or attempted suicide, the midnight torture to the spirits was dispensed with", and the boy was allowed to sleep in his dormitory at night.)

If the boy attempted to run away for a third time, he was dressed in uncouth clothes and, before his assembled fellow pupils, was made to walk round the school hall being 'scourged' by the beadle, after which the boy was put out of the school gates to his friends, if he had any, or to the parish overseer of the poor, if he had not. On one occasion, the ritual had such an effect on the beadle that he was given a glass of brandy to prepare him for carrying out his part of the ceremony. It was always witnessed by two members of the governors of the school, apparently with their approval.

The historical perspective of the treatment of schoolboys in the late eighteenth and early nineteenth centuries was expressed by C Eyre Pascoe, the author of *Dickens in Yorkshire*. Writing in 1912, he records his part of a conversation with an old lady whom he met in Bowes:

> "Dear lady", said I, "when you and I were in our infancy, the schools not merely in Yorkshire, but all over England, were anything but what they are today.

> "You have no doubt heard of Eton, Harrow, Winchester and the like? You probably have heard of Christ's Hospital, for three centuries located in the heart of the City of London? You have heard of England's great public schools undoubtedly? Well, let me tell you that the treatment of boys in some of these schools, a hundred years ago, was anything but what it ought to have been, or what it is now.

> "I myself, when a little fellow, was under a master at a great public school, who was not very different in intemperate speech and brutal use of rod and cane from Wackford Squeers. If the food we had at that school was more varied and better than that provided by Mrs Squeers, it was anything but sufficient. Often and often did I go hungry and supperless to bed. The bullying practised among the boys themselves was hardly less brutal and cruel than that which those of Dotheboys had to submit to at the hands of that educator of youth, its reputed chief: [he whom] Charles Dickens drew, dissected, caricatured, made criminal, and condemned. It was a pernicious and unprincipled system he was bent on exposing and reforming, rather than the heartless character and fraudulent conduct of one indifferent, ignorant, vulgar and ill-tempered schoolmaster in Yorkshire."

3

Yorkshire – and an educational problem

There were private boarding schools all over England, but they seem to have been particularly numerous in one area of Yorkshire. There must have been something very attractive about that county, for in Chapter Four of *Nicholas Nickleby*, Wackford Squeers favourably mentions it five times. This was, apparently, one way of persuading parents to send their sons to his school.

Yorkshire had a reputation for healthy, invigorating air. It was well-known for medicinal and fashionable spa towns, such as Harrogate and Scarborough, and for its moorland and 'broad acres' of rich land and wholesome living. Squeers assures Mr Snawley that, if he sends his stepsons to the "delightful village of Dotheboys, near Greta Bridge, in Yorkshire", they will receive "every wholesome luxury … that Yorkshire can afford."

The schoolmasters in that area had other reasons for choosing Yorkshire as the locality for their schools, but they did not explain those reasons to their potential clients. The north of Yorkshire was sufficiently distant from large centres of population to deter parents from visiting the schools and discovering what they were really like. Parents read the advertisements in the newspapers and met the schoolmasters who went to London, and other large towns, to collect new pupils and convey them to Yorkshire. There are no records of parents themselves delivering their sons to such schools: they sent them on trust. Visits to the schools were very rare indeed, only occurring in unusual circumstances.

The journey by stagecoach from London to Greta Bridge and Bowes was long and arduous but very straightforward; there was no need for passengers to change coaches. The boys and their master came straight up the Great North Road, turned west at Scotch Corner, and went directly to the villages in or near which the schools were situated.

If, as Dickens indicated, the boys travelled sitting 'outside' (that is, on the roof of the coach), the fare was much cheaper. Parents who might themselves prefer to travel inside the coach would have had to pay £6 to go from London to Greta Bridge – a sum of money which would make visiting their sons unlikely, especially as school fees were already just over £20 a year. This also accounts, in part, for the absence of any school holidays which would have involved further outlay in return fares between school and home.

A realistic assessment of these costs can be made by comparing coach fares and school fees with the annual wages paid to two different kinds of workers in roughly the same period. For example, the cost of a return ticket for a seat inside a stagecoach travelling between London and Greta Bridge would have been £12. In Dickens' first novel, *Pickwick Papers*, published in book form in 1837, Sam Weller is paid £12 a year, plus two suits of clothes, to be Mr Pickwick's personal attendant on his travels.

When Dickens was a boy, his father worked as a Naval Clerk and was paid £22 a year – the same as a year's fees at a Yorkshire school. This means that a man had to be very well paid, or to run his own business, before he could send his son to a Yorkshire school – and he might have had to choose between his son's schooling or employing another servant. Indeed, there are signs that those who chose a son's education had to limit their expenditure wherever they could. One group of boys travelled from

Manchester to North Yorkshire in the back of a covered wagon, drawn by four horses and delivering baggage to various destinations. This was presumably cheaper than a stagecoach.

Surprisingly, another cheap method of transport was by coastal steamer. The vessels that took coal from the northern coalfields to London set off fully laden. Having delivered the coal, instead of returning with an empty boat, the skipper would load up with other goods, including passengers. Boys travelling in this way went up the River Tees as far as Yarm (a port capable of accommodating sea-going vessels at that time) and then continued to their school by road. Parents would be unlikely to travel by either of these modes of transport, but were prepared to save money by sending their sons in such ways.

It is quite clear that these people were not rich but were, perhaps, fairly successful businessmen who thought that having sons 'away at school in Yorkshire' would give them some prestige among their acquaintances. Indeed, much of the success of these schools rested on snobbery. The advertisements that the schoolmasters inserted in newspapers emphasised that the pupils were 'young gentlemen' and said 'enquiry may be made of many genteel families.' One schoolmaster (with an establishment in Westmorland, but near the border with Yorkshire) went so far as to claim that he had previously been employed "in the public schools" and had been "tutor to a nobleman's family." Dickens refers with dismal sarcasm to the miserable pupils at Dotheboys Hall as "the young noblemen".

A visit to one of these schools would have dispelled any notion that they were noble, genteel or gentlemanly establishments – but most parents did not pay a visit. They relied on the letters their sons sent them from time to time, at rare intervals, or even annually. Since these letters were censored or dictated by the schoolmaster, they gave nothing but a favourable impression of the school. Here is one letter written from school by Richard Cobden, who boarded at one (if not two) of the Yorkshire schools and later became an eminent politician:

Honoured parents, – you cannot tell what rapture I feel at once more having the pleasure of addressing my parents, and though the distance is so great, yet I have the opportunity of conveying it to you free of expense. It is now turned three years since our separation took place, and I assure you I look back with more pleasure to that period than to any other of my life which was spent to no effectual purpose, and I beg to return to you my most sincere thanks as being the means of my gaining such a sense of learning, as will enable me to gain a genteel livelihood whenever I am called into the world to do for myself.

This letter does not include the address of the school; it is dated 28th March 1817, when the writer was thirteen years old, and is quoted by Lord Morley in his biography of Cobden.

This may seem an improbable letter for a boy of thirteen to have written, but perhaps parents in the early-nineteenth century saw things differently. They may have taken it at face value, and seen no reason to be suspicious about the school their son was attending. Cobden, however, later referred to his schooldays as a desolate time of which he could never afterwards endure to speak. This raises two questions about his letter: was he bravely protecting his parents from the unhappy truth, or was he simply writing what his schoolmaster had told him to write?

Recalling his own schooldays, Bold Cooke wrote, "We were not allowed to send real letters to our parents." Sometimes however, a "real letter" was secretly given to a friendly person, who kindly posted it to the pupil's parents. On at least one occasion, a parent who had received such a letter from a gentleman in a nearby village removed two boys from the school. One unhappy schoolboy had no such means of escape; he later said that his father was not to blame for sending him away to school because, "like many an anxious parent", he unwittingly accepted "the glowing advertisement periodically published in the newspapers." This former pupil added that, to interview prospective parents and gather potential pupils, the schoolmaster in question visited Manchester where, "His grandiloquent account of the academy and his learned staff was not questioned."

In his novel, Dickens makes it clear that some parents were duped into sending their sons to Dotheboys Hall. Squeers reports to his pupils that, on a recent visit to London, he has seen the parents of some boys and "they're so glad to hear how their sons are getting on that there's no prospect at all of their going away." To underline this, Squeers quotes from a letter which states, "Mrs Squeers must be an angel," and expresses the hope that he himself, "may long be spared to carry on the business." This is Dickens' satirical equivalent to the boy's report that his father had been deceived by the schoolmaster's glowing testimony about himself.

There may, however, have been reasons for sending boys away to school other than to enhance their education. Dickens emphasises the number of 'unwanted boys' at Dotheboys Hall. They fell into various categories: the sons of first marriages who were unwanted by their new stepfathers; boys with disfigurements and deformities; and boys who bore signs of having been neglected and unloved throughout their young lives. All these are to be found in the pages of *Nicholas Nickleby*, though there seems to be no recorded evidence for them in real life. Some of these circumstances would be private, of course, but even local people who described the eccentric dress of pupils made no mention of their having deformities. Pupils' own reminiscences do not include these topics either. Perhaps they did not wish people to know that they had been at school with illegitimate or disfigured schoolmates – especially as deformities in a child were often seen as casting a slur on his ancestry. Nevertheless, it seems strange that a circumstance about which Dickens was so emphatic does not appear at all in the accounts given by other people.

Nevertheless, whatever other reasons parents may have had for sending their sons away to schools in Yorkshire, they were expecting them to be educated. To understand why these particular schools should have been chosen, it is necessary to look at what alternatives were available to parents who wanted their children to advance beyond an elementary level of education.

In his second Preface to *Nicholas Nickleby*, Dickens wrote of "the monstrous neglect of education in England." He was thinking of the absence of any national system of education: the first broadly-based Education Act (which applied only to elementary education) was not passed until 1870, the year in which Dickens died. Of course, there were schools before that, but they were largely created by the Church of England and other religious bodies.

There was a British and Foreign School Society (1810) providing Nonconformist education, as well as a National School Society (1811) for the Education of the Poor in the Principles of the Established Church. Despite being called 'British' and 'National', they were not regulated by the country's government and did not, in any case, provide the kind of education for which middle-class parents were looking if they wanted a useful form of secondary education.

There were the Public Schools, but even successful middle-class businessmen and tradesmen could not possibly have afforded the fees. Besides, the Public Schools offered only a traditionally classical education with the emphasis almost solely on Latin and Greek, which made little appeal to most of England's population. There were also some ancient Grammar Schools endowed by funds from wealthy men of long ago, but these schools also concentrated on teaching Latin, Greek and, sometimes, mathematics.

Apart from Sunday Schools and 'Dame Schools' (in which one woman taught children in her own home) there was no choice of school other than private boarding and day schools, which included the Yorkshire schools. Small wonder then, that a survey revealed that forty percent of the population of Manchester received no education at all. In 1840 it was calculated that half the country's population of thirteen to fourteen year old children could not read, and three-quarters of the same age group could not write.

This was the situation that faced parents of middle income who wanted secondary education for their sons. Moreover, they wanted them to be taught something that would be useful when the boys became adults and would help them to make their way in a competitive world. For this reason, they wanted them to be equipped to make progress in the world of business, whether manufacturing or surveying, accounting, or being able to write simple business letters in French.

Parents also wanted a higher moral tone in the schools. This was reflected in the Rules of Woden Croft Academy, and is also satirised in Chapter Four of *Nicholas Nickleby* when, in conversation with Mr Snawley, Squeers claims that his boys will acquire "every beautiful moral that Mrs Squeers can instil".

Lytton Strachey, in his study of Thomas Arnold of Rugby, summarises the situation:

> From two sides the system of education was beginning to be assailed by the awakening public opinion of the upper middle classes. On the one hand there was the desire for a more liberal curriculum; on the other there was the desire for a higher moral tone. The growing utilitarianism of the age viewed with impatience a course of instruction which excluded every branch of knowledge except classical philology; while its growing respectability was shocked by such a spectacle of disorder and brutality as was afforded by the Eton of Keate. "The public schools," said the Rev. Mr Bowdler, "are the very seats and nursery of vice."

It was to attract this new and growing section of the population that the proprietors of the private schools in Yorkshire and elsewhere worded their advertisements. Mr Chapman of Cotherstone offered instruction in grammar, writing, mathematics, arithmetic, book-keeping, geography and French ("by a native of Paris"). Mr Galland of Startforth offered mathematics ("as far as applicable to merchants' accounts") and navigation. The Reverend Mr Wharton of Barnard Castle added to the above items, "mensuration and gauging". Mr Clarkson, at Bowes Hall Academy, included most of the above subjects and also specified "the most useful branches of the mathematics." (He also offered Latin and Greek – perhaps he thought it would add a little social superiority). It is clear that these, and other, schoolmasters were keen businessmen and had realised that there was an increasing demand for useful education, relevant to the contemporary world, in contrast to the old public schools' emphasis on Classics.

EDUCATION,

AT A HIGHLY RESPECTABLE ACADEMY,
COTHERSTONE.

NEAR BARNARD CASTLE, YORKSHIRE,
Conducted, with every due Attention,
By Mr GEORGE CHAPMAN and able ASSISTANTS.

At this Establishment a limited number of (Eighty) Young Gentlemen (there being at present a Vacancy for Ten) from Parents of the first respectability, are Boarded, Clothed, and, without exception, treated the same as Mr. C.'s own Family: also assiduously Taught the English, Latin, and Greek Languages, Writing, Arithmetic, Book-keeping and the Mathematics, Geography with the Use of the Globes, &c.

NO VACATIONS.

Terms, including the above Accommodation, from 20 to 24 Guineas per annum.—Pupils who learn the French Language are regularly attended by a Native of Paris, at 10s. 6d. per Quarter.

All particulars can be had of Gentlemen who, through experiencing kind treatment to Youth, and unremitted attention to instil that Education calculated to qualify them for Men of Business, or Professional pursuits, are desirous to recommend; viz. T. Charlton, Esq. 1, Bell Yard, Doctors' Commons; Mr. Ford, 4, Bagnio Court, Newgate Street; Mr. Hill, Royal Military Asylum, Chelsea; Mr. Dalton, Orchard House, East India Docks; Mr. Penny, 5, Cornwall Road, Commercial Road, Waterloo Bridge; H. Barton, Esq. 18, Suffolk Street East, Battle Bridge; E. Horsefall, Esq. 11, Gloucester Place, Camden Town; or Mr. Greenwood, Agent, 89, Chalton Street, Somers Town.

Mr. CLARK, Mr. Chapman's Assistant, is in Town, and may be treated with from 9 to 12, at Mr. Greenwood's, where he resides during his stay in London: also at the Salutation Tavern, Newgate Street, from 1 to 3 daily.

Each Young Gentleman is expected to enter with 2 Suits of Clothes, 6 Shirts, 6 do. Stockings, 4 do. Shoes, and 2 Hats.

A newspaper advertisement for a Yorkshire school, giving details of its curriculum

Criticism of their severely limited curriculum had been made more than fifty years earlier. William Cowper, in his long poem, *Tirocinium,* or

A Review of Schools, wrote of a parent who sent his boy to a public school: "And is he well content his son should find / No nourishment to feed his growing mind, / But conjugated verbs and nouns declined?"

Despite Cowper's opinion that these schools had "outlived all just esteem," they were still attracting rich parents. On other levels of society, doubts were being felt, and the pupils at 'the great schools' were themselves far from satisfied. The food was insufficient and badly cooked; the boys were locked in their dormitories at night and were only released at breakfast-time; corporal punishment seemed to be the only way in which any attempt was made to keep order, and sometimes the boys (who were up to eighteen years old) rebelled. At Rugby, in 1797, the headmaster's study door was blown open by gunpowder; this rebellion was so serious that troops were called in and the Riot Act was read. There was a rebellion at Eton in 1832, but it was the last at that school; the last recorded rebellion took place at Marlborough in 1851.

Much of the pupils' time was unsupervised. The Duke of Wellington's remark that the Battle of Waterloo was won on the playing fields of Eton seems to mean that boys learned to stand up for themselves in the rough fights that took place within the college grounds, not in the organised games that would be recognised today. William Cowper summed up the matter: "Great schools suit but the sturdy and the rough."

Dr Thomas Arnold, on becoming headmaster of Rugby, saw his priority as the creation of a wholesome, Christian, and gentlemanly tone in his school. He listed his educational aims in this order:

First, religious and moral principles;

Second, gentlemanly conduct;

Third, intellectual activity, which would best be achieved by teachers who stimulated the desire for general learning.

Giving pre-eminence to the first two aims would have pleased the father of Tom Brown, the hero of *Tom Brown's Schooldays* by Thomas Hughes. Although this is a work of fiction, it is closely based on reality and gives a convincing picture of life at Rugby. Hughes was a pupil there during Arnold's time as headmaster (1828-42), so the story relates to the time when Dickens was investigating the Yorkshire schools.

Squire Brown is as keen on proper conduct as any parent who was considering sending his son to a Yorkshire school could claim to be. On the eve of sending Tom to Rugby he ponders his reasons for doing so. He realises that making his son a good scholar is not his main purpose (for neither the Squire nor his wife has any interest in Greek grammar), and concludes: "If he'll only turn out a brave, helpful, truth-telling Englishman, and a gentleman, and a Christian, that's all I want."

Dr Arnold was prepared to widen the range of subjects taught in his school to include some mathematics and French, so some idea of offering a broader education was spreading beyond the private schools. In 1840, a Grammar School Act freed the ancient foundations from some of the restrictions placed on them by the wills of their long-dead founders. These concessions to modernity, whether emanating from Dr Arnold or Act of Parliament were, however, very minor advances compared with the practical, useful, professional and mercantile subjects that were supposedly being taught in the Yorkshire schools.

Both Squire Brown and Mr Snawley in *Nicholas Nickleby* wanted moral guidance for their boys, but only Mr Snawley wanted business studies as well. The reasons for this are clear: Mr Snawley could not afford Rugby and needed his stepsons to make their own way in the commercial world; Squire Brown could afford Rugby and did not expect his son to do other than inherit land in the fox-hunting countryside of the White Horse Vale.

For those of more straitened means and some social pretension, private academies such as the Yorkshire schools were, at least in theory, pioneers in the movement to bring boys up properly and to teach them practical subjects. They were of variable and often deplorable standards, but they were all that was available.

If middle-class parents wanted a moral and useful education for their sons, therefore, there was little they could do other than send them to one of the Yorkshire schools. They may or may not have seen the risks they were taking over their sons' happiness, or their chances of success, but at the time, that was all that England offered.

4

A solution is found in Devon

The problem of finding suitable schools with a broad curriculum at affordable fees was solved by a rector in a rural village in Devon. He was the Reverend Joseph Lloyd Brereton and he was a man with a mission. That mission, as expressed by Jon Edmunds, was "the furtherance of the education of middle England".

Brereton was the son of a Norfolk rector who wrote powerful pamphlets campaigning for improvements in the Poor Law. J L Brereton seems to have inherited his father's zeal, but applied it to education. He was educated at Rugby, where he was unhappy until he went into the Sixth Form under the direct control of Dr Arnold. He took holy orders and, after serving as a curate in Norfolk and in London, accepted in 1852 the living of West Buckland in Devon.

Like his father, Brereton had already begun to write pamphlets in support of his ideas, but now he had the means to put his theories into practice. In his history of West Buckland School, Jon Edmunds writes: "He wished to found an affordable school with a wide, useful education, not a pale copy of the classically dominated public school."

The school which Brereton founded at West Buckland was originally called the Devon County School; it was the first of over a dozen 'County Schools' founded on his initiative. In those days, no schools were organised by County Councils, which were not formed until 1888. The new schools were called County Schools, as each one was situated in a different County. There were, for example, County Schools in Devon, Norfolk, Surrey, Gloucestershire and, eventually, a school which served no fewer than three counties: Northumberland, Durham and the North Riding of Yorkshire; it was therefore called the North Eastern County School.

The first County School began in Devon in 1858, just twenty years after Dickens had exposed the evils of private academies in Yorkshire. It began with only three pupils, but numbers soon grew and within two years Earl Fortescue (a member of a local family who had given strong moral and financial support to the scheme) laid the foundation stone of new school buildings, the school having begun life in a nearby farm building.

The Devon County School, now West Buckland School; from a prospectus of about 1870

Fees were £30 per annum which, Mr Brereton worked out, was a fair charge on a parent who earned £200 a year. Because the school was in a rural area, it was particularly appropriate that the practical subjects should include the science of agriculture. Naturally this involved working on the land, not just sitting in a classroom. However, this did not prevent the headmaster of an academy in nearby Barnstaple sarcastically remarking that instruction in agriculture smacked of the education given by Wackford Squeers. On the other hand, a great compliment to the system was paid by a man who already farmed in the area; Jon Edmunds records that this farmer thought so highly of the scheme that, at the age of twenty-five, he gave up farming for a year in order to attend the school as a pupil.

The academic side of the school flourished: its remarkably broad curriculum included lessons on English law, mechanics, hydrostatics and selections from English literature. The school was recognised by the Oxford and Cambridge Local Examination Boards for its high standard of achievement. These boards were established in an attempt to standardise secondary education on a national scale; in 1865, the Cambridge Board judged that the Devon County School had the highest number of successful candidates of any school in England.

Fees did, from time to time, increase, but faith was still kept with the principle of affordable education. The fees were not fully inclusive and there were 'extras' such as laundry and medical services, but parents of pupils at the Devon County School paid only about a quarter of what Harrow was charging. Sometimes the Devon County School faced financial difficulties, especially in its early years; it could not be a luxurious establishment because its object was to be affordable to people whose incomes could not provide them with luxuries. As late as 1939, the headmaster told parents on Speech Day that they should not expect more than was reasonable for the fees they paid.

Not all the County Schools survived. Most of them were situated in rural areas and were therefore less accessible to parents from industrial or commercial towns, who might wish to educate their sons for a similar way of life to their own. Moreover, Prebendary Brereton (as he became) had, it seems, overestimated the extent to which farmers were interested in giving their sons a secondary education. The Norfolk County School lasted until the late 1880s, but today only two of the original County Schools remain: one was the first to be founded, the Devon County School, renamed West Buckland School in 1912; the other was the last to be founded, the North Eastern County School, renamed Barnard Castle School in 1924.

The North Eastern County School was created after long negotiations to raise money and to ensure a firm constitutional basis for a large boarding school with accommodation for day boys as well. The fundamental principle was that of all the County Schools: moderate fees and sound, broad education. Additionally, these schools provided a considerable number of scholarships, so that even more pupils from the region could be helped to afford the fees.

Very thorough arrangements were made to ensure that the new County School had a secure basis both economically and educationally. People on the first Board of Governors included the three Lords Lieutenant of the north-eastern counties, together with representatives of Durham University and Armstrong College (now part of Newcastle University). Later appointments guaranteed regional responsibility by including as governors local councillors from the counties and towns of the area.

Funds were made available by the trustees of the late Benjamin Flounders of Yarm, who had left a large bequest for the furtherance of education, and the trustees of the former St John's Hospital in Barnard Castle. This was a mediaeval foundation created by the lord of Barnard Castle, John Baliol, in 1229. The charity had, however, fallen into misuse and in 1864 the Court of Chancery had directed that the remaining funds should be used to create a grammar school in the town. That is why, despite Flounders having had almost no connection with the town, the North Eastern County School was built in Barnard Castle.

In round figures, the Flounders bequest amounted to £30,000 and the St John's Hospital Trust contributed £10,000. The Charity Commissioners said that the scheme had to include £10,000 raised by voluntary contributions from people living in the three north-eastern counties. This was quite quickly achieved and Queen Victoria signed her assent to the foundation scheme on 2nd May 1882. All this is a very long way from the often deplorable condition of middle-class education that Dickens had satirised after his visit to Teesdale, but he had prompted the realisation that the situation had to be remedied and this led directly to the creation of County Schools.

The North Eastern County School, now Barnard Castle School;
from a drawing by J H Ludgate, about 1913

Nor was this forgotten when, after three years in temporary accommodation, the school buildings were officially opened at Barnard Castle, in 1886, by the Lord Bishop of Durham, who said:

> Our aims are twofold – to fill an educational gap, and to erect an educational ladder. Mr Brereton some years ago saw this want, stepped manfully forward, showed how the thing might be done and set the example of doing it. The noble institution in which we meet ... is the outcome of that movement.

The 'educational ladder' to which the bishop referred was the process by which children from elementary schools could win scholarships to the

County School, from where they and other pupils could win scholarships to a university.

Fifty years later, at an Old Boys' Dinner on 22nd December 1908, the headmaster of the North Eastern County School made an explicit connection between the past and the present. He was the Rev Francis Lloyd Brereton, son of the founder of the movement, and these were his words:

> It is just fifty years ago that the Devon County School ... was established. In those days boarding schools were of two kinds. There were the great public schools whose fees were prohibitive to parents of moderate means, and there were the private middle class schools in which education was generally far from efficient. The choice was between Rugby and Dotheboys Hall. Fifty years ago a school of a new type was founded which was intended to provide for a moderate fee a really good education, and the name 'County' was adopted as a sort of hall-mark and guarantee that the school was public and honourable in its character, and comprehensive in its aims and that the education was of sterling value.

A couple of words in this extract from Brereton's speech require some comment. 'Public' is used once to refer to the old-established expensive schools, and once to the new and inexpensive County Schools. The explanation is that both types of school were willing to accept anybody's children (provided the parents could afford the fees) from any geographical region and without any religious or sectarian discrimination. The schools were therefore open to the public, so in the broadest sense they were 'public' schools.

Many other schools in England were of a religious foundation and some of them were sectarian. Religion in the County Schools was Anglican, but broadly so. There was no emphasis on sectarian belief or style of worship, and if the parents wished their sons to abstain from communal worship or lessons on a religious subject, they had only to say so, in writing.

The other word was 'comprehensive,' which had not at that time become a technical term for a specific type of school. Mr Brereton simply meant that his school had a curriculum that was wide in content and scope. The North Eastern County School certainly did offer a comprehensive range of subjects. They were grouped under four main headings:

1 English, including religious knowledge;
2 Latin and French;
3 Mathematics; and
4 Science and art subjects, including chemistry and physics, with practical teaching taking place in laboratories, workshops and drawing school.

Other departments included agriculture and engineering. There were experimental plots of ground in which different crops were grown with the application of different fertilisers; visits were made to the cattle market in the town and, less often, to more distant agricultural shows and large farms. Engineering included practical and manual work as well as mathematical calculations; this was found to be most useful when boys who left school at the age of sixteen or seventeen became apprentices in engineering works.

The North Eastern County School had the advantage of being situated in the countryside, but within easy reach of industrial towns such as Darlington (which specialised in railway works), Sunderland and Newcastle (which specialised in ship building). As time passed, a Commercial Class was created to teach book-keeping and other requirements of the business world of the day. The academic side flourished alongside these activities; for example, in 1901 a pupil won an open scholarship to Cambridge University and a former pupil was appointed a Fellow of Durham University.

The early days of these two surviving examples of the County School movement have been described at some length to show how thoroughly and thoughtfully the educational requirements of the middle classes were fulfilled by Joseph Lloyd Brereton and members of his family. They are the heroes of this important aspect of Britain's educational history. Charles Dickens pointed out what was wrong and J L Brereton saw how to put it right.

The Breretons were open-minded men and the spiritual and moral tone of their schools was reminiscent of Arnold's Rugby. It will be remembered that Squire Brown had hoped that Rugby would help Tom to become "a gentleman and a Christian." Dr Arnold himself, according to his biographer, A P Stanley, when seeking a new assistant master said, "I want a man who is a Christian and a gentleman." When the North Eastern County School first entered its permanent buildings, it was announced that Mr Thompson Richardson (a local solicitor and Clerk to the Governors) had given £150 to be invested to provide an annual prize for the boy "who in the opinion of his senior scholars and masters has, during the previous year, best conducted himself as a Christian and a gentleman." Squire Brown would have taken off his hat and cheered, and Dr Arnold might have bowed and smiled his approval.

Eventually, but not until the twentieth century, the idea of teaching technical as well as academic subjects was incorporated into the curriculum of state schools. These were now managed by County Councils – one reason why Brereton's schools stopped using the name 'County School'. By the 1930s, the commercial, engineering, and agricultural classes all ceased to operate at Barnard Castle School, while woodwork classes went on only a little longer. In 1965, the state system created Comprehensive Schools, using the very word that F L Brereton had used in 1908 when describing the aims of a County School. Meanwhile the former County Schools at West Buckland and Barnard Castle continued to concentrate on academic subjects, organised games, the development of character, and the creation of clubs and societies which encouraged aesthetic pursuits and hobbies, and continue to do so.

The whole system of education in both state and independent schools, together with attitudes towards it, has become almost unbelievably different from what it was when, a little over a century earlier, Dickens came to Teesdale and exposed some of the defects of education at that time.

5

What Dickens achieved

Dickens felt strongly that all children should be treated with sympathy, imagination, sensitivity and kindness. When he found that this was not happening, he fiercely attacked the institutions responsible. Workhouses and the Poor Law Amendment Act of 1834 were his first targets, in *Oliver Twist*; the Yorkshire schools, which conducted their business under cover of the "monstrous neglect of education in England," provided his second, in *Nicholas Nickleby*.

Dickens himself did not suggest any alternative system of education, nor did he mention any economic policy for dealing with the suffering of the poor. He was a novelist, not a politician; he passionately cared about what was wrong and, by arousing public opinion, he tried to remove the wrong he had discovered.

The author of an article in *The Westminster Review* for April 1866 did not understand this point. He wrote, "A novel is not the place for discussions on the Poor Law. If Mr Dickens has anything to say about the Poor Law, let him say it in a pamphlet or go into politics."

Dickens chose to do otherwise; he was several times invited to stand for Parliament, but always declined. It would have been difficult for anyone to frame a law for abolishing Yorkshire schools, but Dickens could depict them in fiction in such a damning way that parents would soon stop sending their sons to them and the schools would therefore close. That is what Dickens chose to do and, according to evidence provided by T P Cooper in *With Dickens in Yorkshire*, he was successful.

Local statistics for 1840 show that two schools had recently closed in Bowes and another had moved to Startforth. In 1843 the American author, Francis Parkman, recorded in his journal that the building he identified as Dotheboys Hall was "deserted utterly." So many pupils had boarded at these academies, probably as many as eight hundred, that the closure of the schools had a noticeable effect on the population and the economy of the village.

One surprising feature was that two shops, which had sold buns, cakes and other sweet confections, went out of business. Apparently, pupils had formerly spent their pocket money there. This may seem unlikely, but there are two pieces of supporting evidence: firstly, Wackford Squeers' advertisement in *Nicholas Nickleby* claims that pupils are "furnished with pocket money"; secondly, an actual pupil, William Jones, told the court in 1823 that the younger boys had no soap but what they bought for themselves. They must therefore have had pocket money and, without income from the boys, the shops closed.

Three other shops failed, probably because of the decline in the number of adult customers when the schools closed. No matter how inadequately the boys were clothed and fed, a large number of tradesmen and workers must also have lost their jobs or suffered from diminished earnings. Cobblers, cleaners, laundresses, seamstresses, butchers and farmers, milkmen and bakers (though Woden Croft seems to have baked its own bread) felt keenly the loss of work.

The impact on the economy of the area aroused considerable antagonism towards Dickens and added to a sense of indignation that he had brought to national notice undesirable conditions in a remote rural community.

There was also a strong feeling that the author had acted dishonourably in appearing to make William Shaw (whom local people believed to be the original of Wackford Squeers) the scapegoat for all the schoolmasters who were being satirised by Dickens.

This feeling persisted in people's minds. Over seventy years later, a visiting lecturer booked a room in Barnard Castle's Witham Hall to give a talk on Dickens, with readings from *Nicholas Nickleby*. The occasion was poorly attended. The local man who chaired the event took the opportunity to criticise Dickens for his unfair treatment of Shaw. He claimed that Shaw was not as blameworthy as many other schoolmasters in the district, and had been described by a lawyer as "a respectable man, according to the light of that day". While admitting that the author had been right in "taking up this question of private adventure schools", he accused Dickens from the chair of taking too much notice of malevolent gossip. A subsequent report in the local newspaper quoted these remarks extensively, but entirely ignored the lecturer's performance.

Though local rancour continued to exist into the twentieth century, the really important aspect of *Nicholas Nickleby* was its effect on the Yorkshire schools in the nineteenth century. Conscientious parents who had been deceived into sending their sons to the schools withdrew them, and other parents who might have sent boys there decided not to do so. Dickens had demonstrated that literature can not only entertain, but also influence future events.

Dickens' readers were very numerous and included almost all classes of society. *The Life and Adventures of Nicholas Nickleby* was, like the other novels, first published in serial form and almost 50,000 copies of the first instalment were sold. That was more than any single instalment of *Pickwick Papers*, Dickens' first novel and the one that made him famous.

At a time when evening entertainments included reading aloud to the family circle, it has been estimated that eight people listened to every copy that was sold. Of course, innumerable other people must have at least have heard of the events at 'Dotheboys Hall'. This immensely large audience included many who had taken the story so much to heart that some of them wrote to Dickens asking him not to let Smike die! The author and his public had an almost personal relationship.

The theme of the novel became even more widely known when unscrupulous theatrical producers created plays from it without the author's permission and even, in some cases, before the novel was finished. Later in his career, Dickens travelled widely giving public readings from his works; from 1861, these regularly included "Nicholas Nickleby at the Yorkshire School".

Dickens was so dedicated to the theme of education that he returned frequently to it throughout his works, as the following examples show. In *A Christmas Carol* (1843) two wretched children emerge from the folds of the long robe of the second ghost. The Spirit introduces them to Scrooge:

> This boy is Ignorance. This girl is Want. Beware them both and all of their degree, but most of all beware this boy, for on his brow I see that written which is Doom.

Here the emphasis is on the desperate need for education in general. Elsewhere Dickens portrays individual schools, and by revealing their particular shortcomings shows what was wrong with current educational practice as he saw it.

In *Dombey and Son* (1848) there are two schools. The first is "an infantine boarding school of a very selective description" run by a forbidding lady called Mrs Pipchin. Her system is severe and her policy is "not to encourage a child's mind to develop and expand itself like a young flower, but to open it by force like an oyster." Later, Paul Dombey attends Dr Blimber's expensive boarding school where boys are "crammed" with a variety of topics but never shown the relationships between any of them.

David Copperfield (1850) re-introduces corporal punishment as a feature of education. Mr Creakle entered and "stood in the doorway looking round upon us like a giant in a story-book surveying his captives ... 'This is a new half ... Come fresh up to the lessons, I advise you, for I come fresh up to the punishment'."

In the opening chapter of *Hard Times* (1865), the school depicted has two faults. The first is that the children learn nothing but facts; the children are told: "Facts alone are wanted in life. Plant nothing else, and root out everything else." The second is that the school insists that even a correct answer must be expressed in a prescribed form of words: a horse is, by definition, "Quadruped. Graminivorous. Forty teeth, namely twenty-four grinders, four eye-teeth, and twelve incisive. Sheds coat in the spring…." No children in that school would ever have been asked to describe something in their own words.

From these examples of bad teaching, Dickens shows how he considers the education of children ought to be conducted. Children should be treated as individuals not as a mass audience; children should be encouraged to learn rather than being made frightened to make a mistake; children should be allowed, under guidance, to develop naturally. This continues to be the concern of every generation of teachers and parents.

Of all the schools that Dickens wrote about, the scenes at Dotheboys Hall have made the strongest impression on the public's imagination. The name of this fictitious school has even become an accepted term in the English language for an undesirable institution. Dickens himself might have been surprised at its continued fame, judging by a passage he wrote towards the end of *Nicholas Nickleby*. In Chapter Sixty-Four, we learn that Squeers has been sentenced to transportation for being in possession of a stolen will; the boys at Dotheboys Hall have rebelled against Mrs Squeers, and the school is disbanded forever. Dickens ended the chapter by writing: "in course of time, Dotheboys and its last breaking-up began to be forgotten by the neighbours, or to be only spoken of as among the things that had been."

"The breaking-up at Dotheboys Hall":
illustration by 'Phiz' for Nicholas Nickleby

Dotheboys has not been forgotten, however, and seems destined to be remembered for a long time to come, in ways Dickens could not possibly have imagined.

Nicholas Nickleby was filmed for general release in 1947 and 2003. It was serialised for television in 1957, 1968, 1977, and 1982. In 1980, the Royal Shakespeare Company performed an acclaimed, eight-hour stage version, which opened in London and transferred to Broadway; a video of that production was released in 2004, and further adaptations have followed. Whatever Dickens the novelist might have thought of this, Dickens the campaigner might well have been delighted. It is recorded that he once went to a theatre to see an unauthorised performance of *Nicholas Nickleby*, intending to make a protest to the management. When he had watched the play, however, he decided to make no objection because he felt it had portrayed the true spirit of his book.

Whether on stage, screen or the printed page, Dickens has always engaged the sympathy of a wide audience. Whether he was exposing to public scrutiny the harm done by unregulated and uninspected schools in *Nicholas Nickleby* and other novels, or the miseries of the workhouse in *Oliver Twist*, or debtors' prisons in *Pickwick Papers* and *Little Dorrit*, Dickens helped to create a society which would eventually find such institutions unacceptable.